The Technology of World War II

Sean Sheehan

HODDER
Wayland

An imprint of Hodder Children's Books

THE WORLD WARS

© 2002 White-Thomson Publishing Ltd

Produced for Hodder Wayland by
White-Thomson Publishing Ltd
2/3 St Andrew's Place
Lewes
BN7 1UP

Series concept: Alex Woolf
Editor: Anna Lee
Designer: Simon Borrough
Consultant: Neil de Marco
Proof reader: Philippa Smith

Published in Great Britain in 2002 by Hodder Wayland, an imprint
of Hodder Children's Books.

A catalogue record for this book is available from the British Library.

Sheehan, Sean, 1951-
  Technology of World war II. - (The World Wars)
  1.World War, 1939-1945 - Technology - Juvenile literature
  I.Title II.Lee, Anna
  940.5'4

ISBN 0 750 24019 9

Printed and bound in Hong Kong

Hodder Children's Books
A division of Hodder Headline Limited
338 Euston Road, London NW1 3BH

Picture Acknowledgements:
AKG 10-11, 13, 19, 30, 36-37,
39, 50, 53; Camera Press 25,
54; Corbis 27; Hodder Wayland
Picture Library 6, 7, 43, 47, 57;
Hulton Getty 35, 46, 55, 56;
Imperial War Museum 16, 24,
41; Mary Evans Picture Library
44; Peter Newark's Military
Pictures 4, 5, 14, 17, 18, 22,
26, 28, 40, 45, 48, 49, 52, 58;
Popperfoto 9, 15, 38, 51;
Topham Picturepoint 33, 34,
42; TRH 8, 12, 23, 29, 32.

Contents

CHAPTER ONE

Victories and Defeats

Applied Science

Technology, which is the application of science, has been used in the conduct of war for as long as there has been war. In prehistoric times, stones were sharpened to make lethal heads for axes and spears. Over the centuries, war technology developed mechanical artillery such as large catapults. Later still came cannons, rifles and other machines.

Often, though not always, the side with the more advanced technology has a decisive advantage in war. When the English were conquering Ireland in the sixteenth and seventeenth centuries, their possession of the cannon gun was decisive in taking fortified castles. On the other hand, superior technology did not enable American forces fighting in Vietnam during the 1960s and 1970s to defeat a patriotic and highly motivated guerrilla army.

Horses Versus Tanks

World War II, which began in 1939 with Germany invading Poland, opened with a dramatic demonstration of how superior technology can give one side a vital advantage. The Polish army still used brigades of horsed cavalry whereas the well-equipped German army was spearheaded by a fully mechanized force of sixteen divisions. Six of these, each consisting of 18,000 men, were Panzer divisions, which consisted of tanks accompanied by motorized infantry and artillery.

Laying siege to a city in the late sixteenth century. In World War II, the Russian city of Leningrad (now St Petersburg) was besieged by the Germans for nearly two years.

Panzer Power

Panzer is a term used in the German armed forces to describe its armoured fighting vehicles, especially tanks. Panzer divisions moved at speed, and broke through enemy positions with surprise on their side, with ten more divisions of motorized infantry following up behind in support. They were assisted by air power and it was this combination of ground and air mobility that gave them a fearsome reputation

This kind of attack, called Blitzkrieg (lightning war), used vehicles where horses had once been employed. It had the Poles reeling and within a week their forces were mostly broken up. The ferocious effectiveness of Hitler's Blitkzreig was demonstrated to even greater effect in the following year. In a matter of six weeks in 1940, France, Belgium, Denmark and the Netherlands were overwhelmed by Germany's command of mechanized warfare.

Fleeing in Panic

A German soldier described the impact of the Panzer divisions on the French:

'Civilians and French troops, their faces distorted with terror, lay huddled in the ditches, alongside hedges and in every hollow beside the road. We passed refugee columns, the carts abandoned by their owners, who had fled in panic into the fields.'

Quoted in B.H. Liddell Hart (ed.), *The Rommel Papers*

weblinks

For more information about the Blitzkrieg, go to **www.waylinks.co.uk/ worldwarstechnology**

Part of a German Panzer division, with a large aerial on the tank for radio communication, invading France in 1940.

'The Bomb'

The way in which World War II drew to a close in 1945 presents another example of the way in which technology played a crucial role. The war came to an end in Asia as a result of the development and use of a new type of explosive device that came to be known as simply 'the Bomb'. Scientists discovered a way of releasing the energy of atoms and by July 1945 they were ready to explode an atomic bomb in the desert of New Mexico. The core of the bomb, containing plutonium, was about the size of an orange, but when converted to energy it could inflict enormous destruction on any environment.

The first atomic bomb, dropped on the Japanese city of Hiroshima in August 1945, exploded in the air and released a wave of heat that vaporized people where they stood. Over 78,000 people were killed immediately, and three days later a further 40,000 people lost their lives

weblinks

For quotes from survivors of the atom bomb and photographs of its devastating effects go to **www.waylinks.co.uk/ worldwarstechnology**

An image of the ultimate destructive power of war technology; smoke billowing over Nagasaki after the dropping of the second atom bomb on Japan.

when a second atomic bomb was dropped on the city of Nagasaki. Victims continued to die from their injuries for many years. The total death toll was about a quarter of a million people. Soon after the bombs were dropped, Japan surrendered and World War II was over.

The technology that produced the atom bomb was the result of a sustained period of research by scientists working in secret in Los Alamos in New Mexico. The intensity of the research and development that led to the successful assembly of the bomb was a direct result of the war. A vast plant was built in Tennessee, employing 45,000 workers, 25,000 technicians and many scientists. Working at full capacity, the plant consumed more electricity than the city of Pittsburgh. Such an undertaking was driven by the need to win the war, and the impetus to produce the bomb came initially from the fear that Germany might develop one first. The war forced the pace of scientific advance.

Neutralizing Technology

By the start of the war in September 1939, Germany had developed a magnetic mine that exploded when it came into contact with the hull of a ship. Fitted with a magnetic needle that released the mine when it dipped downwards, the mine rested on the seabed until a ship passed on the surface above. Magnetic forces that are alike will repel one another, and a ship's hull had the same magnetic force as the needle. This meant that when it passed overhead, it caused the needle to dip down and release the mine. British scientists worked out how the mines worked after dismantling an unexploded one, and devised counter-measures that simply neutralized the magnetism of ships.

Looking towards ground zero, the position on the ground directly below the exploding atom bomb, at Nagasaki.

Operation Barbarossa

The role of technology in World War II is not as simple, however, as the replacement of horses by machines and conventional bombs by the atom bomb. Technological know-how is not enough; applying it in the right circumstances is just as important. The course and eventual failure of Operation Barbarossa, the German name for their invasion of the USSR in June 1941, is a good example of this.

weblinks

For information about the planning, implementation and failures of Operation Barbarossa, go to
**www.waylinks.co.uk/
worldwartechnology**

At first, Panzer divisions swept across eastern Europe and advanced 640 kilometres in three weeks. Many hundreds of thousands of Russians were killed or taken prisoner. Within a few months, however, the German forces had to contend with autumn rains, poor-quality roads and a battlefront that stretched for over 1,600 kilometres. A tank that had needed only half a litre of oil to travel 95 kilometres across flat, dry roads in France required 15 litres to travel the same distance across mud-filled sand-tracks in the USSR. The Russian winter exposed the fact that German tanks were not equipped to function in sub-zero temperatures and eventually the army had to rely on hundreds of thousands of horses to pull equipment and supplies.

Technology being literally pushed to the limit by German soldiers as they try to move their motorbikes through fields of mud in Russia.

Another factor affecting the use of technology in war, and one that increased in significance as the German occupation of the USSR continued, is the morale of those fighting. As the German army approached Moscow, not only were its supply lines stretched to the limit but its resolve could not match the patriotic will of Russian soldiers and civilians who were determined to defend their capital city. Technology itself is impersonal but it depends on people to use it and oppose it, and the next chapter looks at the crucial role that people play in applying technology to the conduct of war.

Japanese soldiers in South-East Asia using bicycles.

Pedal Power

Unlike the USA, the Japanese army did not adopt the methods of the Panzer divisions. They continued to rely on horses for transport and built few armoured vehicles. One reason for this was a shortage of oil and, indeed, Japan went to war against the USA and Britain in 1941 because of their embargo that cut off nearly all of Japan's oil supply. Faced with the task of conquering Malaya and Singapore in 1941, the Japanese used 6,000 bicycles, which proved very effective. Landing in northern Malaya and southern Thailand, Japanese troops skirted the dense jungle and many cycled down the 960-kilometre peninsula on roads built by the British in their colony. Colonel Masanobu, a Japanese officer, quipped that the conquest of Malaya was made easy by the combination of expensive British roads and cheap Japanese bicycles.

CHAPTER TWO:
Technology and People

Underestimating the Japanese

People are involved in the technology of war at every stage, from design and manufacture through to the final use of technology in a war situation. At all stages, people's attitudes may play a vital role in its success. The attack on Malaya, which was a British colony when the Japanese invaded in 1941, shows how cultural attitudes can affect decisions about technology.

The threat posed by the Japanese to Malaya was well known before the Japanese invaded and advanced southwards towards Singapore. Malaya was the source of more than half the world's tin and nearly 40 per cent of the world's rubber, and such raw materials were badly needed by Japan. Despite this, little had been done to prepare defences, which reflected the tendency of British officers to view the Japanese as inferior.

After the Japanese landings, two of the British navy's best battleships set off from Singapore to deter the enemy. It was not felt necessary to protect them with air cover and, after being spotted by a submarine, both ships were bombed and sunk by Japanese planes, with the loss of over 800 men. It was the first time a battleship had been sunk from the air. A little over eight weeks later in Singapore, the British general in charge surrendered his army of over 100,000 men to a Japanese army of 30,000. This humiliating defeat of the British is an example of how cultural attitudes and racism can obscure a proper assessment of a country's military and technological capability.

'Sub-human specimens'

The commander of forces in Malaya, Robert Brooke-Popham, had seen Japanese soldiers in 1940 but judged them as racially inferior:

'I had a good close-up, across the barbed wire, of various sub-human specimens dressed in dirty grey uniform, which I was informed were Japanese soldiers. I cannot believe they would form an intelligent fighting force.'

Quoted in Len Deighton, *Blood, Tears and Folly*

Jewish Scientists

The extremely hostile attitude of Nazism towards Jews, which was very obvious after Adolf Hitler came to power in 1933, also had an impact on science and technology. One of Hitler's first measures when he took control was a decree outlawing Jews from Germany's civil service, and this included the universities where research into nuclear science was taking place. The development of the atomic bomb had its origins in the scientific research of European physicists in the early decades of the twentieth century. Many of these physicists, such as Leo Szilard, a Hungarian working in early Nazi Germany, were Jews who fled Europe after 1933.

Szilard left Germany in 1933 and settled in the US, where he campaigned to alert the US government to Nazi Germany's technological abilities. He contacted Albert Einstein, the world-famous physicist, who then wrote to the president of the US warning of the danger of Nazi nuclear science. Einstein was himself Jewish and had also fled Nazi Germany out of fear of persecution. The anti-Semitism of the German government in the late 1930s forced some of the finest European physicists in Europe to flee to the US, where they made a crucial difference in building a bomb that was planned for use against Germany.

Japanese soldiers with a captured British plane in Malaya, December 1941. The British stationed poor quality planes in Malaya because they didn't regard the Japanese as a serious threat.

weblinks

To read Einstein's letter to President Roosevelt, go to **www.waylinks.co.uk/worldwarstechnology**

11

The crew of the B-29 bomber that dropped the atom bomb on Hiroshima; Colonel Tibbets is standing third from the right.

The Morality of the Bomb

The aim of using technology in warfare is to increase the devastation wrought on the enemy. However, many scientists believe that having the capability to cause mass destruction does not necessarily mean it is right to do so. The decision to use nuclear weapons in World War II remains one of the most controversial of the twentieth century.

From one point of view, the physicists who developed the atom bomb are seen as misguided scientists who were used by politicians. Many of the scientists were

'Yes I would do it again'

Colonel Paul Tibbets of the United States Army Air Force (USAAF) has no moral doubts about piloting the plane *Enola Gay* to Japan and dropping its bomb, named 'Little Boy', over Hiroshima in 1945:

'Yes I would do it again if the war situation and the circumstances demanded it …
I didn't realize at the time what effect dropping the atom bomb would have. Our sole aim was to do everything to beat the Japanese. They were our enemies and we were at war. We were patriots and we wanted to see an end to the slaughter so that our soldiers could come home.'

Quoted in www.english.sohu.com

motivated by a heartfelt wish to help defeat Nazi Germany, but their weapon was instead used against Japan. They were not consulted over its use and some of the scientists involved received news of the detonation of the bomb with mixed feelings. One of the physicists, Otto Frisch, recorded feeling 'unease, indeed nausea' as his friends hurried to book seats in a restaurant for a celebratory dinner.

A famous physicist who chose to stay in Germany and work on the development of an atom bomb there was Werner Heisenberg. He was more of a German patriot than a Nazi and later claimed that moral uncertainty about developing such a weapon caused him and colleagues to hold back from more earnestly pursuing the project. This claim has been contested by others, charging Heisenberg with trying to make an excuse for actively working for Nazism. Whatever the final truth, there is little doubt that Heisenberg possessed more moral awareness than some of the scientists who worked for Germany.

Werner Heisenberg won the Nobel prize for physics in 1932. At the beginning of the war he became director of the German atom bomb project, but he and his colleagues failed to develop a workable program for nuclear weapons.

Men Overhead

The technology that allows bombing from the air also allows air crews to distance themselves psychologically from what they are doing. The British writer, George Orwell, thinks about what this means:

'As I write, highly civilized human beings are flying overhead, trying to kill me. They do not feel any enmity against me as an individual, nor I against them. They are 'only doing their duty', as the saying goes. Most of them, I have no doubt, are kind-hearted law-abiding men who would never dream of committing murder in private life. On the other hand, if one of them succeeds in blowing me to pieces with a well-placed bomb, he will never sleep any the worse for it.'

George Orwell, *The Lion and the Unicorn*

Finding the Target

Flying as high as 4.5 kilometres and releasing bombs at the right moment to hit a selected target was limited by the technology that was available in the early 1940s. American scientists developed a bombsight mechanism, called Norden, that calculated the best moment for releasing bombs over a chosen target. Bombardiers in the US airforce attached the Norden to their planes before each mission and it included a self-destruct device so that it couldn't be taken apart by enemy scientists. The Norden, however, was too complicated to be used by every bombardier and it also depended on him being able to see the ground from his plane.

Left An RAF Lancaster bomber flies over the German countryside during World War II.

Right German citizens working to clear the bomb damage caused by bombing raids on the city of Essen.

Bombing Civilians

Just as new technologies can increase intentional fatalities, the limits of available technology can increase the damage inflicted on both the military and on civilians. In the case of the large-scale bombing of German cities from the air, which began in 1942, the British consciously bombed civilian targets. The original policy had been to bomb only selective military targets, but the available technology made such precision impossible to achieve. As a result, the decision was made to change to what was called carpet bombing, targeting large urban areas.

The German bombing of British cities had already taken 30,000 lives by the summer of 1941. Many people felt that some kind of retaliation was necessary to show that Britain had the morale to keep fighting. Air Chief Marshall Arthur Harris, who organized the carpet bombing, argued that it was justified because it helped the Allies to win by weakening enemy morale and disrupting German industry. A stated aim was to 'de-house' factory workers, which would bring about a collapse in the German war industry.

Civilian Morale Stays High

After August 1944, when Allied aircraft no longer faced a threat from German fighters, the selective bombing of specific targets became possible. However, the carpet bombing of civilian areas continued. In total, nearly one million civilians were killed in the bombing of Germany, but the campaign of carpet bombing did not make a crucial difference to the outcome of the war. An important reason why it failed in this respect was that, as with the bombing of British cities by Germany, the morale of the civilian population did not collapse. If technology had allowed for bombers to fly safely over Germany and conduct the precision bombing of non-civilian targets it is likely that carpet bombing would never have taken place. The lack of such technology does not, however, mean that what was done was right.

By 1943, the US air force had joined Britain in bombing Germany.

A Means to an End?

Given that technology allowed for the mass bombing of civilian areas, if this increased the chances of defeating Hitler, was it justified? The idea of a just war, in which the unintended killing of innocent people may occur in order to obtain a greater good, has been used to defend the policy of carpet bombing. However, the campaign of carpet bombing involved the intentional killing of civilians and this is more difficult to defend.

The different opinions about the British carpet bombing of German cities have also been expressed about the firebombing of Tokyo in 1945. General Curtis LeMay, in command of the American air assault on Japan, had a similar strategy to Harris. He ordered a huge raid on Tokyo, which killed about 100,000 people in one night, and raids on other Japanese cities followed afterwards.

Technology for Propaganda

Technology was not only employed on the battlefields in World War II. Radio, which had developed in the years after World War I, was used by all the major war leaders to communicate important announcements to the public and raise morale. In an age without television, the spoken word was an especially powerful weapon and Hitler's emotional speeches were regularly broadcast across Germany. At large-scale public rallies, Hitler made use of the recently invented microphone to amplify his voice and be heard by thousands of people. Special effects were also created at these rallies by pointing huge spotlights towards the night sky, creating a sense of drama and expectation. The cinema was used effectively as a means of propaganda and many fictional and non-fictional films were shot and released during the war years. A famous film made by Leni Riefensthal, *Triumph of the Will*, showed Hitler descending through the clouds in an aircraft in bright sunshine.

An advertisement of 1936 boasts (at the top) that 'All Germany Hears the Führer (Leader)'; the brand name of the radio appears at the bottom.

CHAPTER THREE

Improving the Tools of War

The Tank

Each side in a war uses technology to try to increase its ability to kill more of the enemy. Sometimes, as in the case of the atomic bomb, this resulted in the development of completely new technologies. More usually, existing technology is modified and improved upon in order to increase its destructive power. This is the case with the tank.

The tank was invented by the British and used in World War I. It successfully combined mobility, defensive technology in the form of armour, and the fire power of artillery. The early tanks used in World War I lacked radio contact and a special porthole was used by carrier pigeons to relay messages.

By the time Hitler was ready to launch his Blitzkrieg in Europe, the tank had evolved into a fearsome war machine and its mechanized power seemed invincible. There were accounts of Polish cavalrymen charging German tanks on horseback, waving their swords. This most probably never happened, but the image of horsemen hopelessly charging armed machines captured the sense that the tank represented a new era in warfare. With German tanks advancing on Moscow in 1942, the Russians resorted to using dogs as mines in an attempt to stop them. The dogs, trained to crawl under approaching tanks, were laden with explosives, and a six-inch protruding detonator that would set off the charge.

Tank Parts

A tank basically consists of a hull, a turret and tracks. The hull is the machine's body, home to the engine, fuel, ammunition and human crew. The turret, which contains the gun mechanism, is mounted on top of the hull but with its own ability to rotate. Large caterpillar tracks are attached to either side of the hull.

The perfect tank combines these three elements so as to produce the best combination of speed of movement, strength of firepower and defensive armour. Increasing the size of the gun means a bulkier turret and heavier hull, which in turn means larger tracks, and this can result in a machine that is too heavy and large for its own good. The Tiger weighed 50 tonnes and could support a large gun, while the Sherman was little over half its weight and very mobile, but inferior in firepower. Hitler was fascinated by tank technology and had plans for a massive machine weighing twice that of the Tiger, though it is doubtful how effective such a monster tank would have been.

An American tank modified with a 'rhinoceros' device at the front to help it cut its way through hedgerow-lined countryside after landing on D-Day in June 1944.

19

The Tiger

Tanks played a crucial role in World War II, culminating in the Battle of Kursk in the USSR in 1943. Up to 6,000 tanks, though not all at the same time, were involved in the biggest tank battle in history and it resulted in a decisive defeat for Hitler. His army, which had at first enjoyed spectacular success in the invasion of the USSR, was now on the defensive and the tide of war had turned. The Battle of Kursk involved two of the most successful types of tanks produced during the war: Germany's Tiger tank and the USSR's T-34. The Tiger had armour plating 100 mm thick and possessed tremendous firepower, but it was a new tank requiring constant attention from mechanics, and not enough spare parts were produced.

Tank Women

Russian women were bomber pilots, snipers, machine-gunners and tank fighters in World War II. Here, a German officer describes what happened after a Russian T-34 tank received a direct hit:

'When German tanks approached, it suddenly reopened fire and attempted to break out. A second direct hit again brought it to a standstill, but in spite of its hopeless position it defended itself while a tank-killer team advanced on it. Finally it burst into flames from a demolition charge and only then did the turret hatch open. A woman in tanker uniform climbed out. She was the wife and co-fighter of a tank company commander who, killed by the first hit, lay beside her in the turret.'

Quoted in Patrick Wright, *Tank*

For every ten Tigers only one spare engine and one transmission was manufactured, and this proved insufficient, especially in the demanding terrain of the USSR.

The T-34

The Russians also had a new tank, the T-34, specially designed with sloping armour that could deflect the full impact of enemy fire. It could travel 450 kilometres without refuelling and its wide tracks were an advantage in muddy or snowy conditions. At first though, only the T-34s of company commanders had radios, and messages had to be passed using flag or hand signals. Radios were introduced during 1943 and by the following year Russian tank losses were equal to Germany's, whereas in 1941 six Russian tanks were lost for every German one.

Over 50,000 of these T-34 tanks were produced and they played a crucial role in the defeat of German forces by the USSR.

Guns and Cocktails

The most effective gun of World War II was probably the 88mm gun developed by the Germans. It could be mounted on the Tiger or used separately as an anti-aircraft gun. Against both tanks and aircraft, it fired a shell that travelled at a kilometre per second and one shell could destroy a Sherman.

The Russians had no way of countering the firepower of the 88mm gun but a Russian officer found a way of dealing with tanks that used this gun. Faced with invading German tanks, he ordered 10,000 bottles to be filled with a mixture of petrol and phosphorus, the same mixture used in flame-throwers. The mixture ignited when the bottle broke and the blazing flames spread through the ventilators of the tank. The Germans called these simple but effective devices Molotov Cocktails, after the USSR's foreign minister.

The Sherman

The USA possessed only a few hundred obsolete tanks when German tanks rolled across western Europe in 1939 and 1940. Although not yet at war, plans were immediately drawn up for the design and production of a new tank and the result was the Sherman. Weighing 27 tonnes, the Sherman was fast and reliable, fitted with a radio and an interphone system for internal communication. But it also had weaker firepower and armour plating than German tanks – the Tiger could take out a Sherman at 3.6 kilometres – and the speed with which it caught fire led to it being called 'Ronson', after a popular cigarette lighter.

Comrades in Confined Spaces

Technology can affect human relations, and the limited space that was available inside a tank for its crew is one example of this. The American Sherman tank, for example, had a crew of five and they could spend days together, virtually living inside the tank and sleeping alongside it or even under it at night. The confined space encouraged informality amongst its crew and this became quite apparent when the British used Sherman tanks. The British army tended to insist on formalities, such as the use of surnames instead of first names, and the use of 'Sir' when addressing officers. Such formalities were frequently abandoned amongst Sherman crews as men lived and fought together in close quarters.

The British, who also used the Sherman in large numbers, argued the case for a more powerful gun to be fitted and claimed their proposal was turned down in America because it was a British idea and therefore NIH – 'Not Invented Here'. Later, though, some Shermans were produced with larger guns. Despite its drawbacks, the Sherman proved its worth in Europe, not least because 48,000 of these reliable machines were produced in three years.

Many Sherman tanks, like this one, were produced by Chrysler at a new factory in Detroit known as the Detroit Arsenal.

Hobart's Funnies

Percy Hobart was an inventive British general responsible for adapting existing tank technology to meet the special conditions of the D-Day landings on the defended beaches of northern France in 1944. The inventions were known collectively as Hobart's Funnies. They included an amphibious tank decked in a large canvas skirt that helped keep it afloat. It was steered by propellers driven by the tank's engine. To cope with areas of soft sand, tanks were fitted with a mechanism that could lay firm tracks ahead of themselves. Sherman tanks were fitted with rotors that swirled chains on the ground from a pair of metal arms projecting from the front of the tank. In this way, mines were safely detonated from the onward path of tanks. Some tanks were converted into bulldozers to clear large obstructions, while others had flame-throwers attached for attacking well-defended positions. American planners of D-Day were not convinced by all of Hobart's adaptations but along with the British they successfully used the amphibious tank, known as the Duplex Drive (DD), on D-Day.

One of Hobart's Funnies, an amphibious Sherman tank, being launched as part of an invasion force.

---

weblinks

For more information about Hobart's funnies, go to
www.waylinks.co.uk/ worldwarstechnology

The Spitfire

Powered flight had only been in existence for 36 years when World War II broke out, and Britain's Royal Air Force (RAF) still used biplanes made from fabric and wood. The Spitfire was designed in the 1930s by Reginald Mitchell, who gave it a new Rolls Royce engine called a Merlin. It was made from lightweight metals and some stainless steel.

First flown in 1938, the Spitfire was soon put to the test when the German air force, the Luftwaffe, began bombing England in August 1940. The Luftwaffe's task was to destroy the enemy's air force so that a seaborne invasion of Britain could proceed without the threat of attack from the air. This conflict became known as the Battle of Britain.

The Spitfire had four machine guns fitted to each wing and each gun could fire for about 15 seconds before a new ammunition belt was needed. With this limited firepower the Spitfire needed to fly close to an enemy plane and hope to hit its fuel tank or the pilot himself. At high altitudes, low temperatures could cause the guns to freeze, and Spitfire pilots learned to wrap canvas tape around their guns to help keep out the moisture in the air.

When an order for 1,000 Spitfires like these was placed in 1938 the new factory where they would be built had not yet been constructed.

weblinks

For more information about the Spitfire, go to
www.waylinks.co.uk/ worldwartechnology

The biggest problem faced by existing RAF pilots was in adjusting to the new technology of the Spitfire. These pilots had gained experience by flying biplanes at 320 kph. Now they were required to handle a much more manoeuvrable fighter plane at speeds of around 560 kph. At first, many pilots and their planes were shot down. At one stage the rate of loss was higher than the rate of production of new planes.

The Messerschmitt

The Spitfire faced a formidable enemy in the air, the Bf 109 that was known by the name of its designer, Willy Messerschmitt. Over 30,000 Messerschmitt Bf 109s were produced during the war and their advantage over the Spitfire was the ability to fly at higher altitudes and attack from above. Although it had only two machine guns, mounted on the engine, the wings were fitted with two cannons and a single, well-aimed cannon shot could take out a Spitfire. Bullets from a machine gun could only puncture a plane's metal, but a cannon shell exploded on impact. The supply of shells for a cannon, though, only lasted about eight seconds.

The Bf 109 and the Spitfire had a similar fuel capacity, around 320 litres, but the Bf 109 had to burn fuel flying to its target and this meant it could only remain over England for 20 minutes. The Spitfire also benefited from a high octane fuel that was supplied by America and superior to the fuel in Germany. Radar provided a further advantage for Britain (see pages 40-43) and by September 1940 the planned invasion of Britain was called off because the Luftwaffe had failed to destroy England's air defence system.

The Cockpit

Here, an American writer describes how different the new generation of fighter planes were:

'The cockpit – let's say it's a Spitfire – fits you like a glove. It just about touches your shoulders on either side. The perspex canopy almost touches your head above. You can move your booted feet a few inches in either direction; you can stretch your arms right forward or down, but need to bend your elbows if you pull them back or up. No matter; you can control a fighter with just a few inches' movement of hands and feet.'

Quoted in Len Deighton, *Blood, Tears and Folly*

The Bf 109 was smaller than the Spitfire, making it more difficult to hit. However, with its cramped cockpit it was also less easy to fly.

Mustangs

The limitation faced by the Luftwaffe in the air war over southern England – the limited time the Messerschmitt Bf 109 could fly without refuelling – also presented the Americans with a problem when it came to escorting their bomber aircraft to targets in Germany. The P-38 Lightning and the P-47D Thunderbolt fighter planes could protect the bombers from enemy fighters, but their range was less than 800 kilometres. This meant that they could escort the bombers to and from Germany but could not provide cover for the whole time spent over enemy territory. It was early in 1944 before the P-51 Mustang solved this problem with a range of 1,500 kilometres. If the technology that made this possible had been developed a couple of years earlier, the course of the air war over Germany would have been very different.

The Mustang became one of the best fighter aircraft of the war when its engine was replaced with the Merlin engine, which had proved so reliable when powering the

Against P-51 Mustangs, the Luftwaffe may have lost as many as 1,000 pilots in the first four months of 1944.

Spitfire. The result was a fighter that could outclass German fighters in speed and acceleration. While the USA and Britain could share their technologies, Germany and Japan were never allies in the same close way and they developed their technologies quite separately.

The Zero

The Japanese Zero fighter plane represented a technological breakthrough in aircraft design. Instead of riveting parts together, the wings and the centre section of the aircraft's fuselage formed one complete whole so that the floor of the cockpit was also the central section of the wings. The front and back halves of the fuselage were joined by bolts and this enabled mechanics

'Unexpected speed'

A Japanese Zero pilot described the effect of the Zero's speed:

'It [the enemy aircraft] was a perfect target, and a short cannon burst exploded the fighter in flames. I flashed across the field and spiralled sharply to the right, climbing steeply to come around for another run. Tracers and flak were to the left and right of me, but the Zero's unexpected speed threw the enemy gunners off.'

Quoted in Len Deighton, *Blood, Tears and Folly*

The designers of the Zero were keen to keep the plane as light as possible and selected a particularly small and lightweight engine.

to unbolt the aircraft and gain quick access to its internal machinery. The Zero was very lightweight, giving it a tremendous range of 1,600 kilometres, but this reduced pilot safety because there was no armour protection. The advantage of the extra range was that it helped to keep the aircraft carriers transporting the Zeros well away from where the enemy was being encountered. When Pearl Harbor was attacked in 1941, the Americans had no aircraft to match the Zero.

The Dakota Transport Plane

When the war broke out in 1939, the DC-3 was by far the world's most popular passenger aircraft. Built in the USA, it had the world's first auto-pilot facility, and had been flying for six years when the Japanese bombed Pearl Harbor and brought America into the war. A military version of the DC-3 had been ordered the year before by the USAAF, and over the course of the war some 10,000 were produced.

The British called these planes Dakotas. They became the standard transport plane for the Allies, and although they were not designed to kill, their contribution to the war was enormous. They could transport troops and cargo, deliver paratroopers to a drop zone, or be converted into an ambulance by fitting stretcher berths. The Dakota became the standard aircraft for paratroopers; its sidedoor allowed eighteen men to exit within seconds. Such speed was vital if paratroopers were to land near one another on the ground. In June 1944, nearly 900 Dakotas were waiting in Britain to drop 17,000 Americans and 7,000 British paratroopers into northern France as part of the D-Day invasion.

A Dakota transport plane flies over the Egyptian pyramids.

The Submarine

While the Dakota was a remarkably versatile aircraft, the submarine was used most of the time for one single purpose: to fire torpedoes and sink enemy shipping.

The torpedo was a complicated and delicate piece of technology, a mini-version of the submarine itself, with its own fuel tank, motor-driven propellers, a depth mechanism to keep its position below water and a gyrocompass to maintain its course. Submarines were fuelled by diesel when on the surface, but to submerge these engines were shut down because they needed a supply of air. Electric motors, connected to the propeller shafts and powered by large batteries, were used instead.

The submarine was a dedicated weapon system and little attention was paid to the needs of the crew. The designers of American submarines, more than their British or German counterparts, made an effort to think of the crew's needs, but generally there were few comforts. Toilets could not be used when the submarine was below about 21 metres and washing facilities were at a minimum. Crews used generous amounts of eau de cologne (scented water) to disguise the poor hygiene facilities.

Nazi Germany relied on submarines, called *Unterseeboot* (under-sea boat), or U-boats, in their efforts to win the Battle of the Atlantic. This was an attempt to disrupt the supply of oil and other essential materials transported by sea from North America to Britain and if successful would have altered the course of the war as a whole. In the war in the Pacific, American submarines sank over 60 per cent of the Japanese merchant navy and over a third of Japanese warships.

weblinks

For information on the technology used in the development of U-boats, go to
www.waylinks.co.uk/ worldwarstechnology

A U-boat refuelling. Coming to the surface to refuel placed U-boats in danger of airborne attack. This problem was solved with the development of the schnorkel (see page 43).

CHAPTER FOUR

The Secret War

Secret Codes

The ancient Greek myth of how Troy was captured by hiding soldiers inside a wooden horse is an early example of the importance of secrecy in warfare. The side with surprise on its side has an advantage and World War II was no different in this respect. The Germans began the war with a machine that could turn any message that needed to be kept secret into a coded form. The Enigma was invented by a German, Arthur Scherbius, in 1918, and sold to private companies as a security device.

The Enigma Machine

The figure below shows how the Enigma machine worked, using a simplified version with only six letters. When a letter, for example, 'b', is pressed on the keyboard, an electric current passes through to the scrambler and ends by lighting up one of the letters on the lampboard, say 'a'. The scrambler is encircled by a ring and once a letter has been pressed it turns a notch. So when 'b' is pressed a second time it then lights up a letter other than 'a'. When an entire message had been encrypted it was sent by normal morse code. To decipher the message the receiver also needs an Enigma machine and knowledge of how the scramblers were first set. The receiver, setting his or her machine to the same settings, types in the coded message and the lampboard lights up the letters of the original message. A plugboard, which worked like a telephone switchboard, was also added between the keyboard and the first scrambler. This mixed up the letters before they reached the first scrambler. Without knowing the settings for the scramblers and the plugboard, which could be changed daily, there were 150 trillion possibilities for each letter.

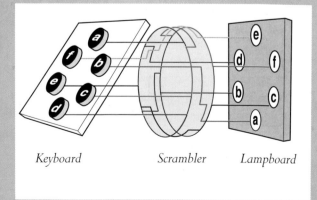

Diagram of an Enigma Machine

Keyboard   Scrambler   Lampboard

A complete Enigma machine like this one was discovered on a German submarine, the U-110, by a British warship in 1941.

Sales were low, because of its high cost, but in 1925 the German government began using them for military purposes. Eventually over 30,000 Enigmas were bought and used.

Poland, fearing a German invasion, made an early start in finding out how the Enigma worked and when war did break out, Polish scientists fled to Britain. Here, building on the Polish work, a breakthrough was achieved with the help of a British mathematician named Alan Turing.

From 1940, the Allies were able to decode Engima messages and the process of gathering 'secret' German messages became known as Ultra. At first only Luftwaffe messages could be decoded, but a lucky break came in May 1941 when a German submarine was captured by the British before the crew was able to destroy its Enigma machine. This enabled Ultra to crack naval messages and in the following year army codes were also broken.

The Germans never found out that their system of encryption had been cracked, although whenever they made changes to their coding the British had to work again at the task of decrypting them. The decoding of Enigma messages made a difference in the Battle of the Atlantic because Ultra was able to pass on to military commanders German messages that came to and from the U-boats. At the same time, the Germans achieved some success in cracking British naval codes; until 1943 they were able to read many Royal Navy messages. They intercepted other transmissions and even managed to listen in on some conversations between the US president, Theodore Roosevelt, and the British war leader, Winston Churchill.

Navajo Code Talkers

The Allies had their own encryption machines that were never broken, but in the heat of battle, especially in the Pacific, the process of coding and decoding could take valuable amounts of time. An engineer, who had grown up on Navajo reservations, came up with the idea of using the Native American language. Messages in Navajo could be entered more quickly than a code, but no Germans would understand what the words meant. Despite the fact that the Navajo were treated as second-class citizens at the time, they were eager to help the war effort and trainees were quickly found. There were difficulties finding words for military terms that had no equivalent in Navajo, but trainees helped solve the problem by using appropriate words from the natural world.

Navajo Code

The list below, in English and Navajo, shows how fish were used for ships, birds for planes, and so on:

Battleship	Whale	Lo-tso
Destroyer	Shark	ca-lo
Submarine	Iron fish	besh-lo
Bomber	Buzzard	Jay-sho
Fighter plane	Hummingbird	Da-he-tih-hi
Bombs	Eggs	A-ye-shi

From Simon Singh, *The Code Book*

An American codebreaker described the Navajo language as:

'[a] weird succession of guttural, nasal, tongue-twisting sounds … we couldn't even transcribe it, much less crack it.'

Quoted in Simon Singh, *The Code Book*

On a Pacific island, two Navajo-speaking Marines transmit a message, safe in the knowledge that the enemy will not be able to understand it.

weblinks

To view a Navajo Code Dictionary, go to
www.waylinks.co.uk/ worldwartechnology

Purple

The Japanese equivalent of the Enigma, first used in 1937, was called Purple by the Americans. Unlike the Poles and British with the Enigma, American intelligence never got their hands on an actual machine to take apart and study. It took eighteen months to work out how Purple operated and success largely depended on gradually identifying repeated parts of a message. Fortunately for American intelligence, Japanese messages were transmitted in the Roman letters of the English alphabet and by 1940 Purple had been broken. The code, however, was changed just before Pearl Harbor and it took another four months to crack the new code.

The value of being able to read Purple communications made itself felt at the Battle of Midway in June 1942, an important naval battle that turned the tide of the Pacific war in favour of the USA. The Japanese plan was to lure American ships away from Midway by pretending to attack another island. Knowing this from Purple transmissions, American commanders practised their own deception by appearing to fall for the Japanese decoy, but then turning back to Midway at a vital moment. The decoding of another Purple transmission allowed the Americans to intercept a plane carrying Isaroku Yamamoto, the Commander-in-Chief of the Japanese fleet, and kill him by shooting it down.

Over a hundred Japanese Zero planes attacked the two small islands of Midway, but the US mid-Pacific base was saved from complete destruction due to the decoding of Purple communications.

Experimenting on Humans

Most of the major countries fighting in World War II conducted secret experiments on human 'guinea pigs' in the field of chemical and biological warfare. The most horrific experiments were carried out by Nazi Germany and Japan, with both countries prepared to kill large numbers of people to test the effects of such weapons. The Nazis used as victims the inmates of concentration and death camps such as Auschwitz. The Japanese set up Unit 731 in Manchuria, where scientists researched the effects of chemical and biological weapons. Thousands of prisoners-of-war were killed in the research.

'Horrendous'

Harry Hogg, who was a British corporal in 1942, recalls the effects of one experiment that used gas on himself and colleagues:

'... *groaning and moaning and crying and oh goodness ... one man in particular, who was a little bit older than I was, was just like an animal. He was trying to eat grass. He was out of his mind. It was horrendous what we went through. Horrendous.*'

Quoted in Rob Evans, *Gassed*

The British tested the effects of mustard gas and tear gases on soldiers in Britain, Canada and India, and the official reports of some of these experiments have still not been released by the British government.

These Polish women at Ravensbruck concentration camp had their legs lacerated by doctors to test the effectiveness of certain drugs on their wounds.

The US carried out similar experiments in their own country, and also in Panama where the environment resembled tropical conditions in the Pacific. The Allies generally shared the results of their research involving human experiments and the scientists saw themselves as contributing to the war effort. Harold Stranks, a British scientist involved in such research, said that doubts about whether or not it was right to use humans in experiments 'did not occur to you'.

The secrecy associated with many of the experiments carried out on humans was in some cases maintained after the war ended. Operation Paperclip was the code-name of a secret American plan that involved recruiting scientists, after the war, who had worked for the Nazis. In 1945, the USA, anticipating possible future conflict with the USSR, was prepared to recruit Nazis who could contribute to American scientific research. The research results of Japanese scientists into biological warfare were also taken by the USA in return for a promise not to prosecute the scientists for war crimes.

'A military secret'

Dr Rascher conducted experiments on the effects of low temperatures on the human body, related to the problem of aircrew trying to survive in the sea. Leo Miechalowski, a prisoner at Dachau concentration camp, survived one such experiment and was told afterwards:

'Everything that has happened to you is a military secret. You are not to discuss it with anybody. If you fail to do so, you know what the consequences will be for you. You are intelligent enough to know that.'

Quoted in Adrian Weale, *Science and the Swastika*

The Allies were keen to recruit German scientists, such as these men arriving in London, to work for them after the war ended.

Chemical and Biological Weapons

The possibility of using chemical and biological weapons in warfare was not unique to World War II. As long ago as the fourteenth century, Mongol soldiers threw plague-infested dead rats over the walls of besieged towns in the hope of spreading disease.

An American programme of research was devoted to toxins such as botulin, produced by bacteria growing in poorly preserved food. Another biological weapon, brucella, was produced in sufficient quantity to kill, in theory, Earth's entire population. The British feared that bomber planes would be used to attack cities with poison gas and nearly 100 million gas masks were

After the war, a US soldier examines a German supply dump of mustard gas shells.

Anthrax

The use of anthrax, a biological weapon that contains the poisonous spores of bacillus anthracis, was considered by the USA, Britain and Japan. The British tested the effects of an anthrax bomb on an island off the coast of Scotland, in August 1942. The chief scientist reported that the effects 'are of a completely different magnitude from those found with chemical weapons' and American scientists came to Britain to discuss the mass production of such a weapon. This led to the establishment of a factory in Indiana and a British order for half a million 1.8 kilogram anthrax bombs. On the island of New Guinea, Japanese forces were captured in possession of anthrax capsules.

produced during the war, including helmets for sheltering babies. Churchill suggested the possibility of gassing German cities but the idea was not taken up by the military.

Deadly Gases

Scientists working for the Allies improved their existing poison gases but did not discover any new ones. In 1936, however, the German military were alerted to the work of Dr Gerhard Schrader, who had discovered a new gas, called Tabun, while working on insecticides. He went on to study an even more dangerous substance, Sarin, and a still more toxic gas called Soman was discovered in 1944. All three substances were nerve gases and worked by paralysing the muscles of the heart and rib-cage so that the victim suffocated painfully. Nerve gases kill within a matter of minutes as compared to conventional poison gases, which take hours to kill.

Germany produced thousands of tonnes of nerve gases. The US army, after tests on an Australian island, wanted to use gas against Japanese-held islands in the Pacific, but the idea was vetoed by Roosevelt. The British had plans to poison German animals by dropping millions of cakes made from linseed feed and anthrax over the countryside, thus creating food shortages.

The main reason that chemical and biological weapons were never used against the armed forces or civilians during the war is that Germany, Japan and the Allies all thought their enemies possessed equally deadly weapons, and therefore no clear-cut advantage would be gained by their use.

The Gas Chambers

Chemicals lay at the heart of the working machinery that brought about the worst crime of the whole of World War II, the Holocaust. This was the plan to exterminate the Jewish race, which caused the murder of six million people.

The people selected for death by the Nazis were primarily Jews, as well as other groups such as gypsies and homosexuals. The order for the extermination of every Jew in Europe was probably given around the time of the invasion of the USSR in June 1941. To begin with, the killings were carried out by hand using guns, but technology on an industrial scale was seen as more effective. Special death camps were built in Poland for the sole purpose of murdering large numbers of people on a daily basis. German technologists came up with various scientific methods for murder on a mass scale.

Ovens, like these at Dachau concentration camp, were built in the death camps to dispose of the gas chamber victims.

weblinks

To read the stories of Holocaust survivors, go to
www.waylinks.co.uk/ worldwartechnology

One method was to construct gas chambers into which were pumped poisonous carbon monoxide fumes, diverted from diesel engines.

At the large Auschwitz camp, experiments were conducted using Zyklon B, a prussic acid produced commercially by a German company as a pest-control fumigant. The manufacturers made it with a distinctive smell so as to prevent accidents, but for the purpose of the Holocaust this warning smell was removed and a Zyklon B version was produced. The experiments were successful and this became the standard means of gassing over one million people at Auschwitz.

Auschwitz employed some 7,000 guards as well as a team of doctors who selected those suitable for immediate gassing and those suitable for the slave labour camps. The administration of the technology for mass killing also required a sophisticated degree of planning, because Jews and other victims had to be transported by train to the death camps from every part of Nazi-occupied Europe. Adolf Eichmann, the high-ranking Nazi in charge of what was called the 'Final Solution' was tried and executed for his part in the Holocaust in 1961.

These former guards at the Auschwitz death camp, photographed after the camp was liberated by Soviet troops, were made to pose with canisters of Zyklon B.

A Technical Problem

German technicians developed gas vans that channelled the vehicle's poisonous fumes back into the airtight interior of the vehicle. Prisoners could be gassed while being driven to a burial site in the countryside. However, the heavy load of people affected the vehicle's stability and an engineer proposed reducing the size of the van's capacity. In his report, a technician deals with the issue as if morality was irrelevant, and refers to prisoners in the van as 'merchandise'.

'The front axle, they [the vehicle manufacturers] claim, would be overloaded. In fact, the balance is automatically restored because the merchandise aboard displays during the operation a natural tendency to rush to the rear doors, and is mainly found lying there at the end of the operation. So the front axle is not overloaded.'

Quoted in Ronnie S. Landau, *Studying the Holocaust*

CHAPTER FIVE

Inventions and Discoveries

Radar

Most of the technology involved in World War II had been developed in the 1930s. Major inventions that emerged in the war were mostly confined to the USA and Germany, because countries like Japan and Italy lacked the scientific and industrial resources to develop new technologies. One important new technology, the use of radio waves to locate enemy aircraft, was developed by both Britain and Germany in the 1930s. Britain was the first to have an operational radar system in place and it gave the RAF a distinct advantage in the Battle of Britain, the air war between Germany and Britain in 1940.

Along the south coast of England, facing the open sea from where Luftwaffe bombers first arrived, transmitter and receiver towers were constructed. Technicians,

An artist's impression of a radar and communications station on the British coast during the Battle of Britain.

40

mostly women, worked at ground level below the towers and their task was to watch for blips on screens. Radio waves were being transmitted across the sky and an echoing pulse was created when a radio wave bounced back from an aircraft in the air. The range of an incoming aircraft could be measured by the time distance between the transmitting pulse and the echoing pulse. The direction of enemy aircraft could be worked out by taking cross-bearings from two other receiving stations in the neighbourhood.

Any information regarding an attack was sent to an Operations Room in London where Luftwaffe positions were plotted on a giant map. Telephone calls were made to the nearest RAF base from where Spitfires and other planes took off to intercept the enemy. The technology did not allow for time to be wasted, because it took a bomber just five minutes to reach the British coast after being picked up on radar.

Women in the south of England, before being posted to an Operations Room, learnt how to plot the course of enemy aircraft at training sessions like this one.

Window of Opportunity

A simple but effective way of avoiding identification by radar lay in a number of aircraft dropping large quantities of small metal strips of paper-backed aluminium. The result was a snowstorm of false blips that confused the radar operators. This technology, called 'Window' by the British and 'Chaff' by the Americans, was also familiar to the Germans who called it 'Dupple'. Neither the British nor the Germans used it at first, because they feared the enemy would work out the technology and do the same to them. The British changed their minds in 1943 partly because they believed that new American technology would be able to function in spite of Window. The other reason was a report suggesting that losses could be reduced by 30 per cent by using Window.

Microwave Transmissions

A later development of radar technology was the use of microwave radio transmissions to identify enemy aircraft. The microwaves were produced by a special device called a cavity magnetron and the British reduced these in size so that they could be carried in aircraft. When this became operational in 1943 it provided the basis for a radar system, called the H2S, that allowed aircraft to detect features on the ground and so help identify a bombing target.

After the Germans recovered a cavity magnetron from a crashed aircraft they were able to develop an airborne system that interfered with H2S and jammed its transmissions. This was a telling drawback to radar and during the last three years of the war Germany and Britain were constantly modifying their radar systems to overcome jamming devices. The Americans developed their own version of H2S, called H2X.

Caught on the surface by Allied aircraft, German sailors can be seen trying to take cover a short while before their submarine is sunk.

Radar at Sea

The Battle of the Atlantic, with U-boats setting out in packs to sink Allied merchant shipping bringing vital supplies from North America, was also affected by developments in radar technology. U-boats could only recharge their batteries on the surface, because air was needed to burn the diesel that provided the electric power, and having to spend a lot of time above surface meant they could be spotted from the air. Allied aircrew could only use their eyes to search for U-boats until air to surface vessel (ASV) radar was introduced. As with H2S, the Germans recovered an ASV set and developed a counter-measure. This led to an advanced ASV set that worked so effectively that Admiral Karl Dönitz, commanding the U-boats, called off his submarine packs in May 1943 until another counter-measure was developed. This did not happen for a year and by then Germany was intent on developing a submarine that could charge its batteries underwater.

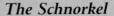

The Schnorkel

German Admiral Dönitz realized that he needed better submarines if Allied supply ships were to be sunk in large numbers in the Atlantic. The schnorkel, a Dutch invention, was put to good use by the German navy in mid-1943. It consisted of two parts, an air intake apparatus and an exhaust pipe for the diesel, which allowed a submarine to recharge its batteries while underwater. This was a tremendous advantage for the German navy because their submarines were always vulnerable to airborne attack while visible on the surface.

A German U-boat, captured in the Atlantic, being brought into a British port. The use of radar significantly increased the number of German U-boats sunk or captured by the Allies.

The V-1

After the USA entered the war at the end of 1941, Germany came to realize that it could not match the American capacity to produce weapons and machinery of war in vast quantities. Hitler was convinced by his advisers that Germany could challenge American industrial might and counter quantity with quality by concentrating on the production of new, advanced weapons. This led to the German air force focusing on the development of a flying bomb, the V-1 as it became known, while the German army developed a rocket bomb called the V-2. Both weapons were known as 'Vergeltungswaffen' – 'weapons of revenge' – hence the abbreviations V-1 and V-2.

It took time, however, to design, test and produce such new weapons and it was the summer of 1944 before the V-1 became a viable weapon to use against Britain. Called a 'buzz bomb' by the Americans because of its distinctive sound, the V-1 flew a little faster than most Allied aircraft and carried a 1,800 kilogram bomb. A gyroscope maintained its stability and the bomb plummeted to earth and exploded when the fuel was cut off over its designated target, the city of London.

This unexploded V-1 flying bomb was found intact by American troops in northern France in November 1944.

More than 2,000 anti-aircraft guns were moved to the south coast of Britain to try and counter the threat from V-1s and Spitfires also tried to shoot them down. Some pilots even attempted to fly close to the V-1 and position a wingtip so as to be able to move the control stick on the gyroscope and send the robot into a sudden dive before reaching its target. Nearly 6,000 flying bombs were launched by Germany and 2,420 of them reached London. Many more would have been deployed but the flying bomb launching sites in northern France began to be overrun by Allied troops by August 1944.

Bouncing Bombs

The Allies decided to try and destroy three large dams in Germany's Ruhr valley by blowing them apart, creating tidal waves that would swamp the surrounding industrial land. It took months to develop a bomb that would skip across the water like a stone and only explode after reaching the dam and dropping an appropriate length down its wall. A specially selected force of 133 airmen from Britain, Canada, Australia and the US set out to bomb the dams and 54 died in the attempt. It took four bouncing bombs to hit the wall before the first dam broke apart and although the floods spread for eighty kilometres and over 1,200 people drowned, the damaged walls were repaired within a few months. The second dam was also temporarily destroyed but the third survived.

The use of bouncing bombs against German dams was celebrated by filmmakers and artists, as shown here in a painting by Frank Wootten.

The V-2

The V-2 was the most complex piece of weapon technology brought to production level by Nazi Germany. It was a rocket, 13 metres in length, using engines fuelled with liquid oxygen and alcohol. Unlike the V-1, when a timer cut off the fuel and it cruised towards its target there was no sound. Londoners, who became familiar with the sound of an approaching buzz bomb, had good reason to feel terrified at a powerful bomb that travelled at such a speed that it arrived before the sound of its passage was heard.

Hitler called the V-2 the 'decisive weapon of the war' and gave priority to its production. Peenemünde, a remote location on the Baltic coast, was the site of the first production plant, but the British learnt of its existence and mounted an air attack in August 1944. A new production plant was then established underground, where thousands of slave labourers from Nazi concentration camps toiled at gunpoint. The atrocious working conditions resulted in 10 per cent of the labourers losing their lives every month.

The technology, however, was new and complex and just over 4,000 were rushed into production during the whole of 1944.

A V-2 rocket being fuelled before launching.

weblinks

For more information about the development of the V-1 and V-2, go to
www.waylinks.co.uk/ worldwarstechnology

Civilians, such as this Londoner being carried to safety, were the victims of V-1 and V-2 technology.

Over 1,000 were launched at targets in England, and about half landed in London. Between them, the 'weapons of revenge' killed 9,000 Londoners. After the war, two of the V-2's chief scientists were recruited by the Americans. They later joined NASA to lead the Saturn project team that made possible the landing on the moon in 1969.

The end of the war in 1945 also ended the work of some German scientists who were developing an advanced form of the V-2 missile that could reach cities on the eastern coast of the USA and explode one-tonne warheads on American cities. Its code name was V-3.

The V-2

A young mother recalled the shock of witnessing a V-2 fall on a Woolworths store in south London:

'*I walked up the road on the right-hand side, with my bag in the right hand and my baby on my left arm. At that point there came a sudden airless quiet, which seemed to stop one's breath, then an almighty sound so tremendous that it seemed to blot out my mind completely.*'

Quoted in Norman Longmate, *Hitler's Rockets*

The Jet

Most of the aircraft that flew in World War II had petrol or diesel piston engines, of the kind still used in motor cars, providing power for the propellers that drove the aircraft forward. In the 1930s, two very different individuals from Germany and Britain independently devised a new technology for aircraft using the turbine.

The turbojet, the aircraft's power unit, used sucked-in air and mixed it with fuel to produce ignition. The expanding gas flew through the blades of the turbine at such a high speed as to create a jet stream. This stream of air, expelled through rearward pointing jets, drove the aircraft forward while the turning blades of the turbine drew in a fresh supply of air. An early German version of a jet aircraft was fitted with the world's first ejector seat because the high speeds created a slipstream that made it dangerous for the pilot to jump clear safely.

Germany was the first to develop a practical jet fighter and by June 1943 the Messerschmitt 262 went into production. Hitler insisted on using it as a bomber, but the weight of bombs slowed it down and cancelled out its spectacular ability to fly more than 160 kph faster than the P-51 Mustang. It was a year before Hitler

Whittle and Ohain

The two men who pioneered the development of jet technology came from very different backgrounds. Englishman Frank Whittle was the working-class son of a mechanic who educated himself in his local public library. German Hans von Ohain had an aristocratic background and studied aerodynamics at university. Whittle's ideas for jet technology were not taken seriously at first, while Ohain, with the support of his university professor, went straight to an aircraft manufacturer, Ernst Heinkel, and signed a contract for the development of his ideas.

Nearly 1500 Me 262 jet fighters were produced but fewer than 150 were actually used in combat.

The Gloster E28/39, the first British plane to be powered by a Whittle-designed turbojet, first flew in May 1941, but the importance of the technology was not appreciated at the time.

reversed his opinion and allowed the 262 to function as a fighter, but by the end of 1944 Germany lacked the resources and the pilots to produce and fly the 262 in sufficient numbers. Allied aircrew who did encounter the 262, however, were shocked to find themselves totally outclassed by this new type of aircraft. Britain's first jet fighter, the Gloster Meteor, was ready by the second half of 1944 but it could not reach the speed of the 262.

German scientists advanced even further with jet technology and, by July 1944, the Me 163 Komet made its first appearance. This aircraft was so fast that a test flight recorded a speed of over 990 kph before the plane stalled and went into a sudden dive. The pilot recovered control, not knowing that he was the first to experience a problem caused by flying close to the speed of sound. The Me 163 Komet pointed the way to supersonic flight but, as with the V-1 and V-2, the technology arrived too late to make a difference to the outcome of the war.

---

weblinks

For more information about the technology behind the Komet, go to **www.waylinks.co.uk/ worldwartechnology**

Flying the Komet

Eric Brown, the first Allied pilot to fly the Komet, remembers the unique experience:

'As you start off on the take-off run under rocket power, it's a very, very fast acceleration and ... at a time in fighter technology when the average contemporary piston-engine fighter had a rate of climb of about one kilometre a minute, this aircraft had an initial rate of climb of 4.9 kilometres a minute!'

CHAPTER SIX:
Did Technology Win the War?

In 1940, the British war leader Churchill wrote that the war would not be won by brute force: 'It is by devising new weapons and above all by scientific leadership that we shall best cope with the enemy's superior strength.' Later in the war, when Germany felt the need to counter America's superior strength, the same argument was used by Churchill's enemy. Albert Speer, a high-ranking Nazi in charge of armaments, convinced Hitler that new technology, based on advanced science, would produce weapons capable of defeating the Allies.

Both sides, then, competed to produce the best quality weapons that technology could provide. This arms race was won by the USA with the development and use of atomic bombs. Their use in August 1945 on two

weblinks

For more information about the Manhattan Project, go to
www.waylinks.co.uk/worldwarstechnology

The two atom bombs dropped on Japan, models of which are shown here, were given names — Little Boy (front) and Fat Man — that provided little hint of their immense destructive power.

Japanese cities, leading to the surrender of Japan some three weeks later, would seem to bear out the argument of people such as Churchill and Speer.

The Race for the Bomb

For the first two years of the war, Germany had the lead in the research and development of atomic weapons. This lead could not be maintained, partly because the field of nuclear science in Nazi Germany was handicapped by the loss of important scientists who were Jewish.

Another reason was that the USA, alarmed at the prospect of the enemy acquiring atom bombs first, set up the huge research plant in New Mexico. Early discussions on the project took place in New York and the plan to produce the atom bomb, called the Manhattan Project, remained highly secret. The best available scientists were recruited and progress was made despite arguments and rivalries between the high-powered physicists.

Perhaps the most vital factor that led to the USA developing atom bombs first was Germany's decision to abandon its own nuclear research. After 1943, Nazism was facing the growing possibility of defeat, and raw materials and other resources became limited in supply. Choices had to be made about how best to use the available resources, and this led to Germany deciding not to pursue the atom bomb project. The USSR had little choice but to abandon its own research into atom bombs after the German invasion in 1941, while Britain lacked the wealth to invest in a research programme and chose instead to contribute to the Manhattan Project.

The scientist Robert Oppenheimer (left) and the soldier General Groves, photographed at the site of a test explosion, were in charge of the highly secretive Manhattan Project.

Science and Politics

Opposing sides, then, competed for technological supremacy in World War II. However, the race for a knock-out weapon, such as the Bomb, is never a simple matter of pure science. Scientists may compete amongst themselves or be affected by their political circumstances. Most importantly, scientists do not usually have a say in final decisions about how, or whether, to use the new technology. The decision to bomb Hiroshima and Nagasaki was taken by politicians and military leaders, not by those who had developed the weapon.

It has been argued that the use of atom bombs did not affect the outcome of World War II. Germany and Italy had surrendered months earlier and by August 1945 Japan was on the point of complete defeat. Others believed that the use of atom bombs would save the lives of

Suicide Technology

The September 11 attacks on New York and Washington in 2001 were not the first to employ technology in a suicide mission on the enemy. The Japanese resorted to using inexperienced young men to deliberately crash their aircraft into enemy targets, usually ships. The pilots and their aircraft were called 'kamikaze', which means 'divine wind', and beginning in October 1944 they sank a total of 34 ships. In the battle for Okinawa, a Japanese island, they killed almost 5,000 men.

weblinks

For more information about kamikaze pilots, go to
www.waylinks.co.uk/worldwartechnology

Kamikaze pilots, carrying Samurai swords, were encouraged to see themselves in the tradition of noble Japanese warriors.

thousands of US soldiers who would otherwise die fighting in the final assault on the Japanese mainland. It has also been argued that American leaders ignored the fact that Japan was very close to surrendering and wanted to use the bomb for political reasons, to keep the USSR out of the Pacific war and demonstrate the superior strength of the USA.

Economic Might

The USA and the USSR were on the winning side in World War II because they were able to mobilize their massive economies in their war efforts. It was their economic power, and their ability to mass-produce weapons of war, that made a decisive difference to the outcome of the conflict. Some of the most important technological advances, such as the jet aircraft, pilotless bombs, and rocket-propulsion, were developed by the country that lost the war. Neither Germany nor Japan, however, could match the sheer quantity of weapons, machines and men that the USA and the USSR could deliver. The Los Alamos plant, for example, had a budget of $2 billion, equivalent to $30 billion today. During the course of the war, American factories churned out one truck for every thirteen soldiers, while Japan managed only one truck for every forty-nine. Early in 1944 one aircraft was being turned out every 294 seconds in the USA.

The American B-17 'Flying Fortress' bomber being mass-produced at the Boeing factory in Seattle.

Conveyor-belt Technology

The USA was especially successful in adapting its peacetime economy for the purpose of mass-producing the machinery of war. The Sherman tank was produced by Chrysler, a car manufacturer, and tanks were also produced by Ford Motor Company on their assembly lines. The conversion of the DC-3 passenger plane into the military Dakota is another example. The Russians were also inventive in mass-producing weapons. When the German invasion threatened its war factories in the western USSR, over 1,500 factories were dismantled and reconstructed in the far east of the country. Over 12,000 kilometres of new railway lines were built to help transport the materials and workers needed for the task.

Very young-looking Russians working on a production line for war planes in Moscow in 1943.

Italy and Japan, both on the losing side of the war, not only lacked the science that could create new technology but, just as crucially, they lacked the industrial resources to mass-produce the machinery of war. Japan forced over a million-and-a-half citizens into war production, working more than twelve hours a day for starvation wages, but could never match the industrial output of the USA and the USSR.

Germany's development of superior weapons came late in the war when the country's economy was suffering from a lack of resources. The V-2 was a potentially devastating weapon but its electronic system could only be produced at the expense of similarly sophisticated equipment needed for radar systems and U-boats. By 1944, Germany was experiencing a fuel scarcity and a shortage of skilled personnel and this contributed to its military defeat. It was too late for Germany to make the best use of its latest, revolutionary technology and in this sense it made no difference to the outcome of the war.

During the war, thousands of women, like this one working on the construction of a Liberty ship, left their homes and traditional places of work to earn higher wages at war production plants.

Liberty Ships

Traditionally, ships were built in one place, one at a time, but William Gibbs overturned convention when faced with the task of producing cargo ships for the USA's war effort. Gibbs was a naval architect and marine engineer and he set about applying the industrial technology of car production to the task of ship-building. Different parts of a ship were constructed in different places, before being brought together and assembled. In total, 2,700 Liberty ships were built in eighteen different shipyards using 30,000 components produced in thousands of factories across the US. Each Liberty ship could carry 9,000 tonnes of fuel and cargo and even one Atlantic crossing was regarded as justifying the cost of construction.

Strategies and Tactics

Technology helped the Allies to win the war because they defeated Germany, Japan and Italy by the military use of tanks, planes, bombs and other weapons. However, as well as requiring the economic power to produce effective machinery of war, the successful use of available technology depends on the skills of the politicians and military leaders in charge. Larger decisions about how to conduct the war, and the best strategy to pursue, may outweigh in importance the actual technology being employed. The success of the Allied landings in Normandy in northern France in 1944 was not guaranteed, especially as the German forces knew an invasion would take place. But they did not know when or where it would occur, and both sides had to try and outguess their enemies.

The D-Day invasion of Normandy in 1944 relied on careful planning and technology for its success.

Operation Bodyguard

Operation Bodyguard was a plan to deceive the Germans into thinking the real invasion force would land at Calais, not in Normandy. Hitler kept tanks and troops waiting in Calais, thinking the landings in Normandy were a trick to distract attention from the real invasion at Calais. The use of these tanks in Normandy could have presented a major problem for the Allies. It has also been argued that the decision in 1942 to invade North Africa instead of northern France was a mistake that prolonged the war. In particular, the British leader in North Africa, Lieutenant General Bernard Montgomery, repeatedly failed to take advantage of valuable information about enemy forces supplied by Ultra decoding of German transmissions.

Victims and Victors

By the end of the war, the supremacy of the US as a world power was signalled by its technological success. The armed forces of the US were not strong in 1939, but by 1945 the country had over 3,000 heavy bombers, 1,200 major warships and sole possession of the atomic bomb.

All the technology of World War II depended on people – from factory workers to the Nazi scientists, and the talented physicists of the Manhattan Project – and it was people who suffered the consequences. World War II lasted for six years and on every day for those six years an average of over 35,000 people died. Three-quarters of those who died were civilians. While many of

Ducks could increase their tyre pressure without having to stop and, once off the sand and on a hard road, could travel up to 80 kph.

The Duck

An excellent example of how American economic strength, combined with inventiveness, played a key role in the outcome of the war is the development of the Duck. Using a new two-and-a-half-tonne truck that General Motors had produced in 1941, the Americans invented a multi-purpose amphibious vehicle that proved highly successful. Its name, following the standard coding system used by General Motors, was D (1942) U (amphibian) K (front-wheel drive) W (rear-wheel-drive) but DUKW was quickly christened 'the Duck' by the soldiers who used the 20,000 of them produced during the war. Ducks were first used on a large scale in the invasion of Sicily, from where they crossed the three kilometres of water to the Italian mainland.

The value of women war workers was celebrated in paintings, posters and a popular song.

the dead were victims of starvation and other natural causes brought about by the war, many too were the victims of the technology unleashed by the countries fighting each other.

Whether it was technology that enabled the Allies to win the war is not, then, a simple question. People play a very important part because they make crucial decisions about when and how to use the technology on their side. The decisions they make are affected by matters that are not technological in nature, like for example, the anti-Semitism that drove scientists to the USA from Nazi Germany, or the Russian winter that the Blitzkrieg's technology was unable to conquer.

Rosie the Riveter

Rosie the Riveter was a propaganda film released in the USA during the war. It was made as part of a campaign to create the image of glamorous women workers who were employed in munitions plants. Rose Will Monroe, who starred in the film, worked at an aircraft factory in Detroit. She had hoped to be one of the women pilots who flew transport missions during the war, but was turned down on account of being a single mother. Like most women workers, Rose was laid off at the end of the war, but found lower-paying work as a taxi driver.

weblinks

To see how women were persuaded to undertake war work, go to
www.waylinks.co.uk/ worldwartechnology

Date List

1933 Hitler becomes Chancellor of Germany. Leo Szilard, a Jewish physicist, flees Nazi Germany.

1939 **1 September** Germany invades Poland.
3 September Britain and France declare war on Germany.

1940 **21 February** The Germans begin construction of Auschwitz concentration camp.
April-June Germany conquers Denmark, Norway, the Netherlands, Belgium and France.
July-September Battle of Britain takes place.
August Secret work begins in a UK research station, leading to the testing of anthrax on the Scottish island of Gruinard.
September Bombing campaign against British cities (the Blitz) begins.

1941 **2 January** The USA announces plans to build the Liberty ships.
9 May A German submarine is captured and an entire Enigma machine is obtained by the British.
22 June Operation Barbarossa, the German invasion of the USSR, is launched.
September Experiments gassing prisoners begin at Auschwitz.
November German advance on Moscow halted.
7 December Japan attacks US base at Pearl Harbor.
8 December Japanese land in British Malaya.
23 December The first military version of the DC-3 passenger aircraft, the Dakota, is delivered to the USAAF.

1942 **15 February** Singapore falls to Japan.
May Start of large-scale gassings at Auschwitz.
4 June Battle of Midway begins.
July The first Sherman tanks produced.

8 November The Allied invasion of North Africa begins.

1943 **16 May** Final preparations made for the use of 'bouncing bombs' on German dams.
4 July Start of the Battle of Kursk.
10 July Allied landings in Sicily by British and US troops.
24 July Allied air raids on German city of Hamburg use 'Window' for the first time.
September Surrender of Italy.

1944 **11 January** P-51 Mustangs are used for the first time in a bombing raid over Germany.
6 June D-day landings in Normandy.
13 June First V-1 flying bomb reaches London from its launch site in northern France.
28 July The rocket-propelled Me163 Komet is used by Germany for the first time.
8 September The first V-2 rocket lands in England.
4 October The Me 262 jet fighter is used in action for the first time.
24 October The first kamikaze missions, against US escort carriers in the Battle of Leyte Gulf.

1945 **13-14 February** Allied bombing raid destroys German city of Dresden.
9 March US firebomb attack on Tokyo.
1 April US troops land on Japanese island of Okinawa.
7 May Germany surrenders unconditionally to the Allies.
16 July First test of an atomic weapon at Los Alamos, New Mexico. The explosion is seen 290 kilometres away.
6 Aug Atomic bomb dropped on Hiroshima, Japan.
9 Aug Atomic bomb dropped on Nagasaki, Japan.
14 Aug Japan surrenders unconditionally to the Allies.

Glossary

aerodynamics the study of how solid bodies, such as aircraft, interact with the air.

Allies the countries such as Great Britain, France, the USSR and the USA that were at war against Germany, Japan and their supporters.

ammunition belt a flexible strip containing machine gun cartridges.

amphibious able to function on either land or sea.

anthrax an organism that can be dried and used as a biological weapon.

anti-aircraft gun a gun designed to be used to attack enemy aircraft.

anti-Semitism prejudice against Jewish people.

armaments military weapons and equipment.

armoured divisions an army grouping consisting of troops and tanks able to work together as a team.

arms race a competitive urge on the part of one country to produce more weapons than another.

arsenal a store of weapons.

artillery large guns used in land warfare.

ASV radar air to surface vessel radar, allowing a submarine to be located from an enemy plane.

biplane an early type of aircraft that has two sets of wings, as opposed to monoplanes like the Spitfire and the Messerschmitt Bf 109.

bombardier the crew member of a US aircraft responsible for sighting and releasing bombs.

botulin a poison capable of being cultivated as a biological weapon.

brigade a subdivison of an army, which formed part of a larger grouping called a division.

brucella a bacteria capable of being produced as a biological weapon.

detonator a device for setting off an explosive.

division an army unit, with its own artillery, engineers etc., under a single command.

drop zone a designated area where paratroopers are dropped from planes.

encryption the conversion of information into a coded form, so as to keep it secret.

Final Solution Nazi name for the programme of systematically eliminating the Jewish race.

firebombing using bombs with incendiary rather than explosive material.

fixed landing gear a plane's wheels and its landing mechanism permanently affixed to its outside, not retractable as with modern planes.

front the front line of an army that is closest to actual battle, or the line of battle itself where fighting occurs.

fumigant a smoke or vapour that acts as a disinfectant.

guerrilla army a small independent force that takes part in irregular fighting against a larger regular army.

fuselage the main body of an aeroplane.

gyrocompass a non-magnetic compass that uses a gyroscope.

gyroscope a rotating wheel that maintains a fixed direction and operates as a guidance device.

Holocaust term used since World War II to refer to the murder of some six million Jews by Nazi Germany.

horsed cavalry soldiers on horseback, as opposed to soldiers in armoured vehicles.

infantry a body of soldiers who fight and march on foot.

interphone system a radio system for internal communication within, say, a tank.

jamming making a radio transmission impossible by causing interference.

jetstream the stream of high-speed gas ejected by a jet engine.

kamikaze Japanese suicide pilots and their aircraft.

Luftwaffe the German Air Force.

Malaya the country stretching from Thailand to Singapore, now part of modern Malaysia but under British control in 1941 when it was invaded by the Japanese.

Me163 Komet the world's first jet engine aircraft; Me stands for the designer's name, Willy Messerschmitt.

munitions military weapons, ammunition, stores and equipment.

P-51 Mustang American fighter aircraft; the 'P' stood for 'pursuit'.

plutonium a radioactive element used in nuclear technology.

prussic acid a highly poisonous liquid, also known as hydrocyanic acid.

repulsion the force by which something repels, or drives back, something else.

slipstream a current of air driven back by a plane's propeller.

snipers those who fire shots from hidden positions, usually at long range.

Soviet Union another name for the USSR (see below).

strategy the art of moving troops and weapons into the best positions.

toxins poisons produced by living organisms.

transmission in a motor vehicle, the mechanism that transfers, or transmits, power from an engine to the axle.

turbine an engine driven by a flow of water, gas, steam or wind.

Ultra The British intelligence unit responsible for decoding enemy messages.

uranium a radioactive element used in nuclear technology.

USAAF the United States Army Air Force, which became known as the US Air Force after the war.

USSR the Union of Soviet Socialist Republics (also known as the Soviet Union), of which the most powerful state was Russia.

ventilators openings for the circulation of air.

Sources and Resources

Further Reading

Battle Stations, Taylor Downing and Andrew Johnson, Pen & Sword Books, 2000. This book, with lots of illustrations and fascinating facts, looks in detail at some of the decisive weapons of the war, including the Spitfire, the Dakota, and the Sherman tank.

Blood, Tears and Folly, Len Deighton, Pimlico, 1993. A readable account of the early years of World War II, including examples of how all the sides used available technology.

World War II Battle Plans, edited by Stephen Badsey, Helicon, 2000. Lots of maps and explanations of the role of technology in over twenty battles.

Other Sources

William B. Breur, *Secret Weapons of World War II,* John Wiley & Son, 2000

Rob Evans, *Gassed,* House of Stratus, 2000

Guy Hartcup, *The Effect of Science on World War II,* Macmillan Press, 2000

Ernest Mandel, *The Meaning of World War II,* Verso, 1986

Robin Neillands, *The Bomber War,* John Murray, 2001

Richard Overy, *Why the Allies Won,* Jonathan Cape, 1995

Clive Ponting, *Armageddon,* Sinclair-Stevenson, 1995

Simon Singh, *The Code Book,* Fourth Estate, 2000

Adrian Weale, *Science and the Swastika,* Channel Four Books, 2001

Patrick Wright, *Tank,* Faber & Faber, 2000

Places to Visit

Imperial War Museum
The Imperial War Museum
Lambeth Road
London SE1 6HZ
Tel: 020 7416 5000

National Army Museum
Royal Hospital Rd
Chelsea
London SW3 4HT
Tel: 020 7730 0717

Websites

http://motlc.wiesenthal.org/pages/t009/t00913.html
Photos, maps and information about the Blitzkrieg.

http://history1900s.about.com/library/weekly/aa072700a.htm
Contains quotes from survivors of the atom bomb and photographs of its devastating effects.

http://cobweb.washcoll.edu/student.pages/karen.sieger/war/war.htm
Provides details of the origins of Operation Barbarossa, its implementation and its failures.

www.usisrael.org/jsource/biography/einstein.html
Information on the German Jewish scientist Einstein and how he was treated in Nazi Germany.

www.dannen.com/ae-fdr.html
Albert Einstein's letter to President Roosevelt warning him about the possibility of Germany developing the atom bomb.

http://web.inter.nl.net/users/spoelstra/g104/subjects.htm
A site dedicated to the Sherman tank.

www.dday.co.uk/page42.html
A site dedicated to Hobart's Funnies.

www.sciencemuseum.org.uk/on-line/flight/flight/spit.asp
Information about the Spitfires.

www.wpafb.af.mil/museum/tours/etop51.htm
Details of the development and impact of the Mustang.

www.uboat.net/technical/index.html
Information on the technology used in the development of U-boats.

www.history.navy.mil/faqs/faq61-2.htm
Information on Navajo Code Talkers in World War II, including a Navajo Code Dictionary.

www.auschwitz.dk/id3.htm
Contains stories of Holocaust survivors.

www.theotherside.co.uk/tm-heritage/background/v1v2.htm
Provides details of the development of the V-1 and V-2.

www.aviation.nmstc.ca/Eng/Collection/sd082e.htm
Information on the technology behind the Komet.

www.atomicmuseum.com/tour/manhattanproject.cfm
Contains detailed information about the Manhattan Project.

http://motlc.wiesenthal.org/pages/t037/t03716.html
Explains the recruitment process for kamikazes and displays photographs of kamikaze pilots.

www.nara.gov/exhall/powers/women.html
Explains how women in the US were persuaded to undertake war work.

Index